To Gerry,

Enjoy!

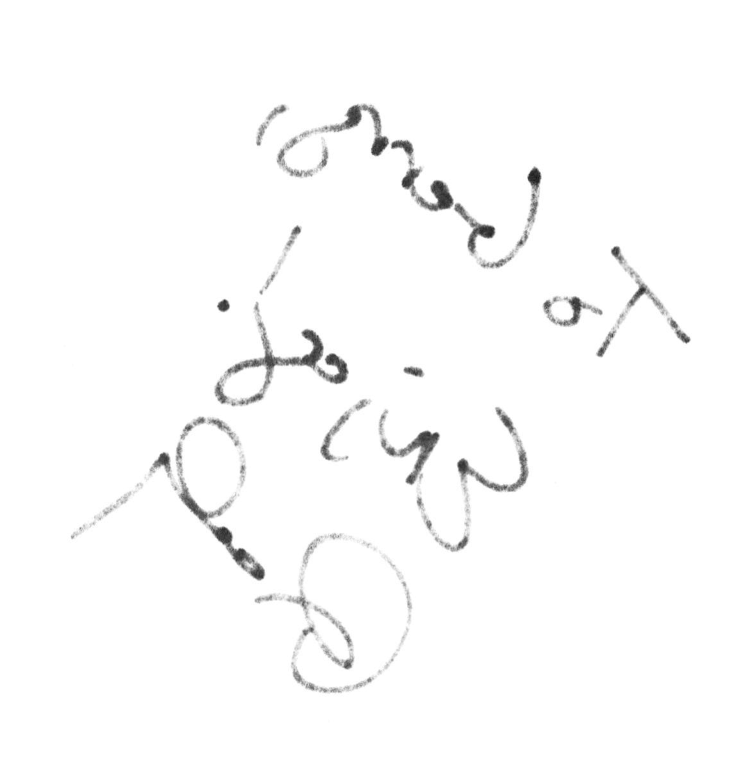

The Power of Habits

How to Become a Rainmaker

Are your habits taking you from where you are today to where you really want to go?

Randy Schuster

The Power of Habits
How to Become A Rainmaker
by Randy Schuster

ISBN: 1-58570-001-0
Published by Indaba Press
A division of Indaba, Inc.
11125 8th Street East
Treasure Island, FL 33706
www.Indaba1.com
For bulk orders please contact (727) 360-0111

Printed in the United States of America

Rochester, NY 14604
(585) 546-1656
Fax (585) 546-6575
www.CoordinatedPlan.com
www.ThePowerOfHabits.com

“I have never met anyone with a better understanding of what it takes to be successful – or with the knowledge and energy to make it happen. If Randy had been around 100 or so years ago, he would’ve perfected the automobile, not Henry Ford.”

Rick Woodson
Journalist
Rochester, N.Y.

"Habitual behavior is a commercial virtue. Discipline is the hallmark of service. Randy provides very clear and immediate steps for creating a flourishing, productive practice. Anyone hoping to conduct themselves successfully in business would benefit from reading Randy's illuminating and thoughtful book."

Garrett D'Alessandro
CEO Rochdale Investment Management
New York, NY

“Randy’s methods have set him apart from his peers, and he has grown his business in ways most people just dream of... Allow him to share his thoughts and ideas with you. I'm sure you'll be able to integrate some of his methods. “

Ira D. Jevotovsky
Re/Max Realty Group
Pittsford, NY

“If you believe one of the important precepts of life is growth, this book should be a requirement to manage and create your own development. A true professional who practices what he preaches, Randy has dissected the many steps and strategies, which create lessons, and insights that, can be taught to anyone no matter what walk of life.”

Jay Mulein
Managing Partner   Diversified Financial
Los Angeles, CA

“More time cannot be produced and Randy’s habits show us how to make the most of the time we have.”

Richard Croce
CEO Viking Industries
New Paltz, NY

“I have known Randy for ten years and have experienced how he has put into practice these habits. He not only talks the talk, he walks the walk."

James Cerone, CLU, ChFC
Centra Financial Group
Rochester, NY

Dedicated to
Erni, Danny and Matt

Special thanks to- Kris Dussmann, Delia Costanzo, Sharon Rollins, Marie Eizenarms, and Jim Cerone for your wisdom. Without all of you none of this would have been possible. To my editor, Rick Woodson, thanks for your perspectives. Exceptional thanks to my mentor, and friend, Hellen Davis.

Table of Contents

Forward

In the 1930s, the life insurance industry created a scientific process to teach its agents how to turn their sales jobs into a business. One of the hallmarks of the industry is that those in sales freely shared the sales cycle process with all who were interested in growing their business. In turn, many sales people in the insurance industry have shared these time-tested processes with their clients and those in other industries, therefore spreading these concepts to be applied in other fields. As a result, the life insurance industry has produced some of the most successful and influential sales people in the world.

The industry has changed greatly since the governmental walls between insurance and investments came crumbling down in the late 1960's and early 1970s. Many who had previously sold only life insurance were suddenly attracted to selling investments. Because life insurance has to be sold, many backed away from selling insurance and began to focus their careers on investments, partly because of the perception that it is an easier product to sell, and that there is less rejection involved. Thus, the result is what we know today as the financial planning community. Life insurance companies also became enamored with selling investments as a means of growing their businesses and the industry as a whole gradually began to stop investing in training and development of new sales associates to enter the field. Because of the enormous transition, these tried and true techniques became a lost art.

I began my insurance career in 1995, after being part of a successful third-generation family business that ultimately gave way to the chain-store revolution. I have studied these methods and with the advent of technology, I have updated them so anyone can use them to build a successful career regardless of the industry they choose to enter. It is my sincere pleasure to give back to those who seek similar knowledge to grow their business to the next level. Good luck.

Introduction

No matter what industry or type of profession you we are in – doctor, lawyer, dentist, accountant, insurance or financial professional, retailer, manufacturer, etc., or any number of other career choices, one thing is for sure: It's all about bringing in new business and just as important, servicing the existing customers, clients, patients, etc. we have worked so hard to attain. Even the purists of the "classic salesperson" are not really in a sales job. Actually, they are all running an independent business if working by themselves or a business unit within a large company or structure.

In the following pages, I will explore a number of techniques, thoughts, philosophies and strategies on how to take your business to the next level. I have read more than 75 books researching the topic and have spent over 1000 hours with numerous trials and errors to successfully refine these methods so they can be implemented on a practical basis. You will learn how to track your activities and numbers in a more methodical manner and how to apply this information into your business practice to increase your production. You will learn how to use your time in a more effective manner through several methods. You will learn how to spend less time working and earn more income.

Transferable ideas include strategic use of specific language patterns to implement while on the telephone or in an appointment to take you to the next phase of the selling cycle, implementation of time-tracker software to analyze how much time is spent in front of the client and your hourly rate. What is unique about this age-old topic? I will share activity charts that illustrate detailed information accumulated over the past decade. This will include the number of calls made for new prospects, yes's and no's, data, presentations, sales, referrals, completed interviews, and more.

I will also share an example of an actual inventory chart with typical average size cases, aging (number of months case is open), total potential revenues, actual closed cases, etc. We rarely see this type of specific information. Finally, I will give an example of how uses of specific language patterns employed while successfully calling for new appointments and use of key power phrases so you can take your sales process to the next phase.

This book is intended to be useful and practical. Even those who wish to focus on one concept are able to go to a specific chapter and immediately apply the methods discussed to their own business.

The Habit of Activity

"You've got to ask! Asking is, in my opinion, the world's most powerful and neglected secret to success and happiness." Percy Ross

I'll never forget the first week of January 1995. I had been training for three solid months to get to that week, when I would begin my new, wonderful career in the financial services industry – A.K.A., the life insurance business. My manager insisted that before I began I must gather more than 2,000 names, each recorded on a separate index card. I had to rubber band packets of

50 cards each and he explained it would take approximately one hour to get through 50 cards. He instructed me that the only way I would come into the business would be by cold calling, that I was not to call on people I already knew. He said that if I did this religiously for a couple of years it would be much easier in the business. So, at 8 a.m. on Wednesday, January 2, I began. I called all day long, until 5 p.m. and secured three appointments. You see, it was my goal that day to get at least three. And I did.

The next morning while driving into the office, a thought crossed my mind: "I must be crazy," I said to myself. "Why would anyone come back for another day of this?" I had just spent eight hours and all I got was three appointments. Well, that self-talk didn't do me much good. At around 9:30 on Thursday, January 3, I had one of those bad experiences. You know, the one we've all had, where the prospect on the line gets very angry with you, saying, "Why are you calling, what are you doing this for?"

Well, I almost broke down. My manager had taught me to never hang up the phone. He said you would have one hour to go through a packet of 50, take a 15-minute break and then get back to the phones. When that call was over, though, I didn't put down the receiver. Instead, I closed my eyes and the very first thing that flashed through my mind was my 2-year-old on the floor of our dining room – which had no furniture, I might add – and I thought, "I can't stop I must continue. I have a family to feed." So I continued to go through my stack of index cards, but I did not get any appointments. My goal for Day 2 was to get five appointments. As I walked into the lunchroom, a veteran 25-year agent said to me, "How did you do this morning?" I said, "Butch, I didn't get any

"You will never achieve big results in your life without consistent and persistent action."

The Power of Focus

appointments." He looked down. His face changed color and I knew what he must have been thinking, "Boy, that is tough. I would never want to do this." And then I said, "Butch I am very proud of myself. No, I did not get any appointments this morning." Then, I told him the story of the irate prospect and I said, "I am proud of myself because I made it through the morning."

Well, that little bit of self-talk worked wonders for me. That afternoon, between 1 p.m. and 2 p.m., I made two appointments, and between 2 p.m. and 3 p.m., I made three more. I was elated. I had achieved my goal for the day. At the end of that day, my manager came in and asked, "How are you doing"? I told him I had seven appointments in two days. And he said, "Great! The record in one week is 20. Go for it!"

"46% of all salespeople ask for business one time. 24% ask two times, 14% ask 3 times, 12% ask 4 times. Only 4% of all salespeople ask the same person for their business 5 times...which represents 60% of all business sold."

The Aladdin Factor

Well, on Friday I secured four additional appointments, so for the three days I had 12, and I was in business. I kept doing this day after day and soon, I didn't have to be on the phone 11 hours a week anymore. It went down to nine hours a week, then eight, and so on. My manager said I should schedule between 12 and 15 new appointments every week, week in and week out.

At the end of March I walked into my manager's office and said, "Joe I have a problem." He knew I was doing well on the phone. He said, "Come on in, Randy." "What's up?" I said, " Joe we start the month of April on Monday. I have completely filled up the next five weeks with new prospect appointments. I have between 12 and 15 appointments for the next five straight weeks. What do I do?"

His response was, "Well, you better double book." I cringed, but of course, he was right, because many of those appointments cancelled. That was okay. The point is, Just Do It!

"Perseverance is a great element of success. If you only knock long enough and loud enough at the gate, you are sure to wake up somebody." Henry Wadsworth Longfellow

As a result of that unpleasant phone call back on my second day, when I closed my eyes and visualized my child on the unfurnished dining room floor, that night I went home and asked my wife, Erni, to go to Sears and get a picture of the kids so if I ever get down, it will remind me of what I had to do. Today, 10 years later, that picture is still prominently displayed in my office.

In the early days, when I would get down, all I would need to do was to look at this picture. My kids were 5 and 2 at the time. This was the reason I had to continue to phone even though I did not like it. The telephone is a necessary evil.

"Activities are the underpinning of everything we do."

Tony Gordon

I look back on that first year when I dialed the phone 12,520 times, and I averaged about five and a half hours a week on the phone. That was comparable to coming in every morning and making calls from 8 a.m. to 9:15 a.m., five days a week and having the rest of the day to see clients. That didn't sound too bad. In retrospect, it was not too high of a price to start my business. As you will see, the habits I learned in those early days still carry over today and apply to any business, big or small, and are applicable to all industries.

The Habit of Time

"The proper function of man is to live, not to exist. I shall not waste my days in trying to prolong them. I shall use my time." Jack London

The famous saying, "Everyone has two things in common: death and taxes," should be amended to read, **"We all have 24 hours per day, 7 days per week, and 365 days per year. The key is how effectively we use this time and this is what makes us unique.**"

There are a number of techniques one can implement to make the most of every day.

1. Early in my career when I was going from one meeting to the next and it came time to design the case, I couldn't remember what had happened in the previous interview. There are usually two or three weeks between meetings, depending on the time of year. So, I decided to get a Dictaphone and religiously summarize what happened at a meeting within 15 minutes after its completion. This allows for the greatest detail to be captured and be reviewed later. Also, it's not just the recanting what occurred during the meeting, but it helps to clarify which tasks your staff members will be assigned. After taping the notes of a meeting, I do not see the file again until after each staff person has completed their assignments. Then it is returned to me in presentation form for my review.

This significantly reduces the amount of paperwork involved and maximizes the time spent either in front of clients, thinking about whom to see next, or being on the phone with clients.

2. Have your assistant screen your calls so that you can control whom you talk to and when. This also will eliminate the unsolicited and marketing calls we all receive that do nothing but waste our time.

3. When on the phone, especially when you are making appointments with new prospects, I routinely turn on my "Do not disturb" button and I tell my assistant, no interruptions, even from my wife, unless it is an emergency. In addition, I turn off my email so that I have no excuse to do anything other than make the calls during the allotted time.

"Don't wait. The time will never be just right."

Napoleon Hill

4. Whenever possible, people in the financial, insurance or real estate industry should refer to friendly advisors, especially attorneys who are familiar with your work. Knowing how they operate and what they are going to say will save you time and also may help you in closing your sale.

5. Choose an hourly time rate that you are worth and do not accept any cases or clients below that number, unless on an exception basis. Let's say you feel your time is worth $300 per hour. If you bring in a case, you should be able to estimate the amount of time it is going to take you to complete. For example, you may estimate that a straightforward contract or agreement may take ten hours to complete. Based on those numbers, you should see at least $3,000 in revenue. A more involved case may take between 25 to 50 hours, depending

on its complexity. You should make sure you are going to be compensated accordingly.

6. This one may sound simple, but it is incredibly important. Purchasing up-to-date computer equipment means that your assistants will be able to process the cases much faster and their turn-around time will be much quicker. A small investment of $1,000 to $1,500 in computer equipment saves me tens of thousands of dollars in staff time. Computers are very reliable employees that don't talk back, ask for raises or take vacations. My assistants have a 17" flat screen monitor that provides comfort and gives them space on their desk. Also, make sure you stay current with all software.

7. Recently, with the advances in computer technology, we have begun to aggressively scan all client documents to a paperless office environment. This

allows instant access by my staff and as they have reaffirmed, is much more efficient than having to get up and physically find the file. Implementing an electronic filing system is not nearly as expensive as you may think. You might even consider hiring high school students, who are technologically apt and are likely to do the work for less money.

8. Other than attorneys and accountants, who are paid for their time, how many of us actually track our own time – that is, what did we accomplish during the day? How much time did we spend in front of our clients and customers? At the end of every day, I dictate whom I saw and why. For example, I can tell you over the past five years all the business I did, by year, in front of clients and what my per-hour rate worked out to be. This is an important step in analyzing your daily production.

We are all busy, but are we effective with the time we choose to work? I break down my activity into two broad categories: Client Contact Time and Not In Front of Client Time. The latter includes travel time and vacation time. As you can see by the chart below, I have worked 7.7 fewer hours per week and all but 1.5 hours of that coming from time not spent in front of the client and travel time. And by the way, my leisure time increased by 12 days.

Time Analysis

Comparison of 2004 vs. 1999

(Activities By the Week)

	2004	1999
Client Contact Time	13.0	14.5
Not in Front of Clients Time	19.9	23.2
Travel	5.2	8.1
Total Per Week	**38.1**	**45.8**
Vacation	**23 Days**	**11 Days**

"How you spend your time is more important than how you spend your money. Money mistakes can be corrected, but time is gone forever." David B. Norris

By consciously tracking my time over the past five years, I have reduced my driving from 38,000 miles to 19,000 miles, which translates to over three hours per week – or, put differently, 150 hours per year. My vacation time over those five years has gone from 11 workdays to 25 workdays. And my time not in front of clients has gone from 23 hours to 19 hours, which is over 200 hours per year. It doesn't take much to accomplish this. For me, taking advantage of the bountiful software programs available today has been a tremendous tool. I simply taught my assistant how to use it and all I have to do is dictate the information.

The Habit of the Calendar

"Just see the people." Bruce Etherington

I'll never forget going to Chicago in 1998 for my first Million Dollar Round Table (MDRT) conference. MDRT represents the top 5 percent of financial and life insurance producers in the world. One must earn the right to be a member based on annual production levels set by the roundtable. I was intently listening to Karl Hartey, who at the time was only seven years into his business. His former career was an 18-hour-a-day dairy farm helper. He was approached to come into the life insurance business with the promise that he would only have to work 14-hour days. In 1997, he had achieved 444 completed sales the previous year and by June of 1998, he was already in MDRT's exclusive Top of the Table club, which consists of the top one-half of 1 percent of financial professionals. To give you an idea of what 444 paid sales means, the industry average is 25 per year. A typical roundtable member does 100 cases in a year's time. This was a remarkable feat.

Having been in business now for a little over 10 years, I still phone new prospects every week. It is an appointment on my calendar that cannot be canceled. My assistants know they are not allowed to remove this self-imposed mandatory appointment from the calendar or move it to another part of the week without checking with me first. The calendar is completely booked for the next 12 months with new-prospect phone time. Every Wednesday at 9 a.m., I begin to make the calls. It only takes about an hour, but I get it done early and get it out of the way so that I can move on to other things. I can't emphasize how important it is to make sure you see new prospects every single week. In addition, I still maintain a calendar of 12 to 15 client appointments per week, and that does not include time spent with management or industry functions. I also make sure that at least two weeks out that the calendar is at least half full. That is, seven or eight appointments, and three weeks out, at least three or four appointments. This is part of my routine, week in and week out all year.

"Winners are those people who make a habit of doing the things losers are uncomfortable doing." Ed Foreman

"Destiny is not a matter of chance, it is a matter of choice; it is not a thing to be waited for, it is a thing to be achieved." William Jennings Bryan

The Telephone

As previously mentioned, every Wednesday morning beginning at 9 o'clock, I phone for new appointments. As Marvin Feldman, the legendary son of the greatest life insurance salesman ever, the late Benjamin Feldman, once said:

"I hate to prospect. I know how to prospect, and I do it very well. Just because I don't like it doesn't mean I don't do it. I force myself. The difference between someone who is moderately successful and someone who is very successful is that the successful individual does all the things that the other person doesn't really want to do. So I send the letters; I make the phone calls; I do all those type of things. I don't like it, but I do it" By Marvin Feldman CLU, ChFC

I still hate it, but - it is a necessary evil. I have learned a number of techniques on how to make the process easier and more efficient. When I receive a referral from a client, I routinely ask them to contact the prospect for me and tell them a little bit about me and to expect my call. I always start the conversation with, “Mr. Prospect he (the referrer) said you are a (great guy, good tennis player, very good friend, etc.) And he said we should get together.” Here are some examples of what I mean.

"Do the thing you fear and the death of fear is certain."

Ralph Waldo Emerson

1. I was having lunch with a client a few years ago, the day after the Super Bowl and he said, "Randy, last night at 11:30 p.m. after the game I went out snowmobiling." To put this into perspective, it had snowed about five or six inches the night before and it was about 20 degrees outside. So I said to my client, "What? Are you nuts?" Then he shared with me that he wasn't alone and he went with someone who was on my target list. I took the opportunity to ask my client if I could meet with his friend. Of course, he said he would be glad to refer me to him. So when I called the prospect the conversation went something like this; "Hi Jeff, I was having lunch with Steve the other day and he told me that you guys went snowmobiling after the Super Bowl and as I recall there was about five inches of snow and it was

about 20 degrees outside. Are you guys nuts?" This evoked a laugh and I continued, "Steve also said that we should meet." Jeff immediately said yes and only at that point did I say, "My name is Randy Schuster and when can we meet?" That phone call turned into business.

2. Dan had been on my target list for approximately six years. In fact, he didn't realize it, but I had called him three previous times – once a cold call and the others from a referral that didn't end up going anywhere. This time, however, I waited for the right referral, from a very close friend of his, before I made the call. So when I followed up with my client about the referral, I called him on his cell phone and he happened to be at the beach in South Carolina, he said he would immediately call Dan and tell him to expect my call. A few minutes later I called Dan and

said, "Dan, isn't it great that our mutual friend took the time to contact you while he was on the beach during his vacation?" This also evoked a laugh and then I asked for the appointment. Dan is now a client.

3. A client told me about being at his office and telling his peers that he had just come back from his attorney's office, where he was executing a new will with his financial advisor. One of the people he worked with overheard this and said, "I've got to meet that guy." When I called him, I introduced myself as the guy who took his co-worker to the attorney's office and he immediately knew who I was and he made the appointment with me. He is also a client now as well.

"Do the thing you fear to do and keep on doing it...that is the quickest and surest way ever yet discovered to conquer fear."
Dale Carnegie

"I have a lot of things to prove to myself. One is that I can live my life fearlessly."
Oprah Winfrey

The point here is, get to know something about your prospects and their relationship with the person who referred you. That is, let them bond. When I speak with a potential client, I always say something about them and the referrer first before introducing myself. That way, they have good thoughts about their friend and are less likely to be on the defensive dealing with me, especially if they get hounded with calls on a fairly regular basis. This approach has greatly increased my success rate of converting referrals into appointments.

"Rejection hurts today as much as it did 35 years ago, although today I just became incredibly wealthy for taking it." by Tony Gordon

The Habit of Keeping Score

"Comfort zones are plush lined coffins. When you stay in your plush lined coffin, you die." By Stan Dale

Do you remember when you were brand new in your career and your manager would ask you every week about your *vital statistics*? In sales, no matter what industry, it's the same basic formula: How many appointments did you have? How many referrals did you get? How many first-appointment interviews did you give? How many follow-up interviews did you have to collect the customers' criteria? How many presentations did you make to ask for their business? How many sales did you achieve? And, what was your sales volume?

Many of us tracked that information when we first started our careers, often because our managers told us we had to. But as we became successful we slacked off. Many people in sales stopped keeping these vital statistics after 10 years in the business. I was very careful not to fall into that trap. I have found this information to be fairly easy to keep track of by using a spreadsheet.

I break things down into key categories. For example: How am I doing on my telephone time? As I mentioned earlier, during my first year in the business I made 12,520 phone calls, which averaged out to approximately 44 dials per hour and about 5 hours and 45 minutes per week. In my first year 1,371 people said no, they would not see me and 365 said yes, they would see me. That is how I built my business. As a tribute to all of those no's, I kept those index cards, more than 1,000 of them, standing tall in a prominent corner of my office. When people ask me about this, I tell them how I came into the business, and the cards are a constant reminder that I need to do the things that others don't like to do, and that includes me, in order to be successful.

By contrast, during 2003, I spent on average less than one hour per week phoning. Total dials: 670, and 98 people said they would see me, and 28 said no they would not see me. Or, put another way, over 71.4 percent (70 of 98) first-time prospects were seen. The numbers worked out to more than two yes's per hour, compared to 1.29 when I first started. It is also very efficient because I know that the time I spend phoning is resulting in appointments.

As a symbol of success, I have kept over 1000 cards where prospects had refused to meet with me.

"The results of your bad habits will not show up until much later. Where are your habits taking you?"

Les Hewitt

Telephone Time Example

Year	Hours / Week	Total Dials	Dials /Hr	Total Yes	Yes /Hr	No	Spoke with /Hr	% of Yes
2004	0.7	515	14.15	97	1.15	37	2.94	91%
2003	0.9	670	14.23	98	2.09	28	2.69	78%
2002	1.2	602	9.65	73	1.17	28	1.62	72%
2001	1.20	862	16.58	109	2.10	29	2.21	79%

"Sales are not lost by a wide margin, it's the small stuff. Sales are won slight edges." Glenn Mattson

New Business Contact Activity By Year

Year	New Appts.	Appts Kept	# of Yes	% of Opens	Cases Presented	Cases Sold	Success Rate	Referrals Obtained
2004	97	60	45	75%	89	61	69%	152
2003	98	61	40	66%	100	68	68%	157
2002	73	65	49	75%	68	60	88%	160

Another example is tracking front-end activity by year as you can see by the chart above.

Retailers must constantly bring in new merchandise to sell, evaluate their products to see what is hot and know when to mark down old inventory that is not selling. How much new business do you have in the pipeline right now – active open cases with documents? In the financial industry, often we need to see clients' last wills and testaments, tax returns, insurance policies, and investment statements. It is crucial for the client to gather and send you information before the second appointment (sometimes you can even get clients to bring their documents with them to the first appointment) because it allows your staff to prepare you for the appointment to have a better understanding of the client's situation, ask more thought-provoking questions, and most importantly, shows commitment from the client that they are sincere about your potential business relationship. What does your current inventory look like? How long does it take, in months, by the time you open a case until it is completed and paid for? How much of your business comes from new clients compared to existing clientele? What is your average sale per case? Again, it is fairly simple to compile this information with an Excel spreadsheet by listing all of these things and doing some simple calculations.

Current Inventory Pipeline

Client	Cat	Date Opened	Date Sold	Total	New/Old Client	Hours	Hourly Rate
Client 1	A	8/20/2003	1/20/2004	8,438	New	8	1,055
Client 2	B	10/10/2003	2/1/2004	1,500	Old	4	375
Client 3	B	11/26/2003	2/15/2004	-	New	9	-
Client 24	B	2/5/2004	5/15/2004	600	New	1	600
Client 25	B	3/25/2003	5/15/2004	1,050	New	3	350
Totals				98,003		186	526
Ave				3,920			
25							
Average time **all** cases in months			3.93				
Average time **new** cases in months			4.31	77,583	79%		
Average time **old** cases in months			3.12	20,420	21%		

"Your habits will determine your future."
Jim Rohn

Tracking and knowing this activity information allows one to see their weaknesses and show where improvements can be made. It enables you to run your business model more efficiently and helps to challenge you to move your business to the next level.

The Habit of Referrals

"Rich people are different in a very specific way-for them referrals are a way of life." by Moshe Hadari

The continued gathering of referrals is the secret to success in any business. Keeping a good flow means I have a consistent practice. My motto is, **"I get one quality referral every business day. It's easy – I am a referral machine."** Do I always get this? Not all the time, but if I don't think that way, then I do not get them at all. The old saying, "You get what you ask for," definitely applies. I always ask for business owners and individuals with high net worth. I am actively calling on approximately 30 prospects at any given time. How many do you have in your referral bank? There are a number of concepts you can use to get more referrals and enhance your reputation:

- Build a prospective client profile on referrals. Harvey Mackey, author of *Swim With The Sharks*, developed a system called Mackey 66, which allows you to build a database of prospects you haven't reached yet. Following his method, when you finally do meet the prospect, it allows you to know an awful lot about them, build rapport quickly, and use this information to your advantage. I've adapted his concept to my business and have built a database with more than 200 prospects with background information on each of them. Background information is easily found in local business journals and newspapers. Today, it is not difficult to go on the Internet to get information. Sign up for access to archives in your local business journal and have the ability to do research and get information about prospects and/or a company you are trying to get in to see. I've delegated this task by hiring someone to do the information gathering for me. All I do is supply the list of names and read the individual profiles.

- When I started in this business years ago, I was taught to get an endorsement letter on the clients' stationery. I found this to be very time consuming. Also, you give up control because you have to get the endorsement letter signed within a reasonable time frame, which can be difficult. I've since started using my own short letter, which allows me to be in control. It reads something like this:

Dear Mr. Prospect:

Last week I met with your friend John Smith and he suggested that we get together. I will be calling you next week; so that we can spend 5 minutes on the phone to both determine if there is a reason to meet.

Cordially,

Randy Schuster

Cc: John Smith

Now I control when the letter is sent out and by sending a copy of the letter to my client, if I am unable to reach the prospect, here I have a reason to call my client and ask for help. He or she is usually more than willing to call the prospect to get them moving in the right direction.

"No matter how small and unimportant what we are doing may seem, if we do it well, it may soon become the step that will lead us to better things."

Channing Pollock (1880-1946) Playwright and lyricist

- Years ago, MDRT suggested that we submit our names to the local newspaper business section, along with a photo, stating that we've just come back from the annual roundtable meeting. I've done this every year since – it's free advertising – and boy, does it get a lot of attention! Also, I put my name in the paper for company awards, such as "Leader of the Year," National Quality Award, and anything else I can think of. I can't tell you how many times someone will come up to me and say they saw my name in the paper for some award. This obviously applies to any field, whether it is a realtor winning an award or attending a convention, a dentist getting a specific type of training, etc.

- For the past three years, I have organized a client-appreciation night/party. I rent out a suite that holds 100-plus people at our local minor league baseball stadium and treat my clients and their spouses/guests to a night out. Why do I do this? Typically, my 'A' clients do not attend this type of function, but my 'B' and 'C' clients do. They can see my face, know who I am and address any issues they might have. It's important that from their prospective, I am servicing them. It's a very good way to get in front of 100 people and treat them to a good time with very little effort in a good comfortable atmosphere. It's a great way to keep their business on the books and those customers coming back for more.

The Habit of Communication

"To exist is to change, to change is to mature, to mature is to go on creating oneself endlessly." By Henri Louis Bergson

In the 1970's, John Grinder and Richard Bandler discovered the science of predicting a person's pattern. This became known as Neurolinguistic Programming- NLP for short. **It is important to note that using powerful NLP with someone should only be done for the right and ethical reasons.** For me, learning and working at becoming a better communicator – verbal and non-verbal – has translated to a much quicker sales cycle process. It builds immediate trust with the client and helps ensure that you will keep their business. There are three types of communication skills one must learn to master: non-verbal, oral and written.

The easiest to learn, and the one most people stop at is the non-verbal. A common technique is to mirror and match a client. The purpose of this skill is to quickly build rapport with the prospect. The quicker you build rapport, the faster you can move through your sales process. You can use similar voice tones and inflect your voice as needed to make a point. You can also use mirror and matching to test whether a concept you have proposed makes sense to the prospect. For example, if you present an idea and want to see if your prospect agrees with it OR accepts it, pick up your coffee cup and take a sip. If your prospect *follows* you and also picks up their drink, then you can move forward to the next part of your presentation. Try to test your mirror and matching twice before closing and moving on to the next phase. If you don't, you risk losing the sale. The mind and body are linked and you may not realize your loss until much later, even for days or weeks. Invariably it can be traced back to that moment in time when the prospect did not buy into what you were saying at the time. This has helped me to read what a client is thinking and therefore anticipate my next move. It has allowed me to influence clients and their advisors to move the sales process forward. It has also helped to build a connection quickly and to establish a relationship.

A more difficult task is to improve your language patterns in order to influence others. By using words effectively, we can bypass resistance and create mental activity in other people's minds. I have built my own arsenal of power phrases and words to use with clients. Let's analyze some examples of how these phrases are designed to influence someone.

> "*Just suppose <u>we spend the next 10 minutes and both brainstorm</u> as to who might be a good candidate?" by Randy Schuster*

This is a professional way to ask someone to be open-minded. *We <u>spend the next 10 minutes and both brainstorm,</u>* is another way to ask the other person to do something, and *who might be a good candidate,* is in this case what you are asking for, a new referral.

> *"Term insurance equals a band aid" by Larry Clayton, CLU*

> *If you procrastinate, then the cost to just fix this will go up by 5 percent. Just suppose your best suppliers said their costs were going up, you would <u>make the time</u> to <u>figure out a way</u> to <u>just implement the plan before</u> the price increase.*

The above phrase is loaded with any number of combinations you can use. *Procrastination* is a major problem for most people. Here we have attached a value-system issue in that the products will cost more. As you can see, I used a second phrase, *just suppose*, followed by several phrases that are underlined, and finally reinforcing the importance of keeping the price down.

For good measure, here are a couple of additional examples:

"How do you feel about your business partner's widow, her next husband and their attorney who will be here at your office every Friday for 50 percent of the profits?" by Tony Gordon

"What do you remember about your grandparents?" by David Solie (MDRT 2004)

"You wonder why I push you...I deal with the exception not the general rule." by Hellen Davis, CLU

Creating and practicing power phrases like those will help you move to the next stage of the selling cycle.

The art of the written word is similar to oral, and can be a very powerful influencer. The old saying, "I will believe it when I see it," couldn't be more true when a well-drafted letter is read by a prospect. Many times this can be accomplished by giving the prospect a choice. For example, if your goal is to set up a new appointment with someone, try the following.

> *"You can meet with me next Tuesday at 1 p.m. or next Thursday at 9 a.m."*

Does it really matter when you meet, Tuesday or Thursday? Generally not, what is important is that you secure the appointment. You can improve your odds of securing the appointment by attaching a value-system statement – that is, something important to them. For example, if you know that their last will and testament is 10 years old, you can add:

> *"Because you told me how important it is to protect your family in the event that you die now."*

This will get their attention, since their family is the most important thing to them in the world. This statement also brings this event to the present by adding, "*You die now,*" which creates a sense of urgency that they must make the appointment right away.

I have used letters on a number of occasions to influence clients to take the next step forward. Often I will hear a comment from another advisor on the team, such as the attorney, who says that for years they tried unsuccessfully to get the client to come in and they were pleased that we were finally able to convince them to get the documents completed.

Whether you use non-verbal, oral or written techniques, the end of the sales process should always include a future pacing statement. Tell the person what will happen next, even if this may cause a certain amount of stress. As an example, in the investments business, if you replace an advisor the client has had for 10 years, that advisor is sure to fight to keep the relationship. This will occur without you even knowing it. Prepare the client for the inevitable call. On occasion, I have even suggested the client call the advisor and tell them what they are doing and why. This will save you time in the future and you will avoid having to resell the client and rebuild the hard-earned trust you fought so hard to gain.

The Habit of Strategy

First you have to figure out what you want. Second, you have to decide that you deserve it. Third, you have to believe you can get it. And, fourth, you have to have the guts to ask for it."

By Barbara De Angelis

What is your niche?

When I first came into this business, I decided I needed a plan. How was I going to be different than all the other people I would be competing with? What would make me unique so that someone would prefer to buy from me instead of the competition? I determined that I would be a comprehensive financial planner, kind of like a coach of a sports team. That would allow me to create rapport and gain their trust. Sometimes, I get a part of the business now and I have set the client up for the future sale. Another important and often over-used phrase is "give great service." I also believe it is critically important for you or a member of your staff to return telephone calls within 24 hours. This gives the client a reason to be loyal. That is, you're providing great service, which will keep hard-fought business on the books.

Client Commitment

There is a widely held perception in the financial planning community; one must see clients at night. Initially, I thought this to be true. When I first came into the business I would get to the office by 8 a.m., work until 5 p.m., go home, eat dinner, shower, shave, spend a few minutes with my kids, and then exhaustedly rush out the door for a 7:30 appointment, getting home at 9:30 and repeating the same thing the next day. After three months, I made the decision that if what I do is so important then I am not going to do nights anymore. I decided to tell my prospects that my last appointment begins at 5:30 p.m. in the afternoon. I don't think that anyone ever turned me down and if they did I didn't want them as a client. In 1998, three years into the business, I was tired of doing four nights a week. Therefore, if somebody wanted to see me at 5:30 p.m., I would do it on a Monday so I could get it over with for the week. My business actually increased because clients respected this. Since 2000, I have not had a night appointment.

All of my existing clients are accustomed to this, but what do you do when a new prospect says, "I work during the day and will only see you at night or on the weekends." I use the following language pattern: "Mr. Prospect, my business hours are 8 a.m. to 5 p.m. All of my clients work during the day. I have three options for you: I can see you at 8 a.m. or I can see you for a working lunch in my office and my assistant will order lunch in advance for us so that we can make our time efficient, or I will see you at 3:30 in the afternoon. I do not do nights and I do not do weekends. Which of those three would you like to do?" I have never once had a prospect refuse to make an appointment because of this. In fact, I believe this shifts control of the appointment back to me, where it belongs. After all, we can choose who should be our clients.

"Risk more than others think is safe. Care more than others think is wise. Dream more than others think is practical. Expect more than others think is possible."

West Point Cadet Maxim

"All who have accomplished great things have had a great aim, have fixed their gaze on a goal which was high, one which sometimes seemed impossible...

Orison Swett Marden

Leverage and Delegation

When I was 14 months into the business, I was buried. I had many cases open and not enough time to properly prepare for them – and I had no money – yet I knew I had to invest in my business. I observed my business-owner clients, many who had debt. It dawned on me that if I wanted to grow my business, I had to get a loan. So I called my father and said, "Dad, I need $4,000 – I just hired my first assistant." Before I could get that sentence out of my mouth he quickly responded with, "When are you going to pay it back?" Well, that was February and I just blurted out, "December," not knowing that I would just end up writing him a check before December and not telling him that I was going to send it. Boy, was he proud! I also went out and secured a home equity line of credit for $25,000 on my house. I never quite used that much, but just knowing it was there was a tremendous stress relief.

My assistants are top notch. I can't stress enough how important it is to be very picky about whom you hire. And when you find that right person, don't be afraid to pay them at the high end of the wage scale. You will find that quality assistants will save you time and aggravation so you can focus strictly on getting the business and taking care of it, allowing your assistants to handle everything else. Once you have accomplished this, the next phase is to bring in a junior producer so you can carve out your smaller clients and turn them over, and to focus more on new business and servicing your top clients.

Be consistent and you will have less stress

In the life insurance industry, there is an inordinate amount of business written in the fourth quarter. And then comes the first part of the year and very little business is written. I have never had this problem because I've always picked an average quarterly target of how much new business I want to put on the books. For example, you might want to set a goal to sell $25,000 of new business each and every quarter. It becomes the bread and butter of your business and does not include any large cases, but that alone will reduce stress.

The Habit of Thinking Big

"What one-sentence inscription would you like to see on your tombstone that would capture who you really were in your life?"
Jim Loehr

What is your purpose in life? What do you want to be remembered for? Too many people spend their days with no particular goals, no ambition. They just seem to shrug and take life as it comes. Why is it most of us put limitations on our abilities, desires, the goals we have, the places we want to go, the amount of income we want to earn, the amount we will save, etc.? Why is it that we pass this limited thinking down to those who we hold most precious, our children? Thinking big is the most powerful, yet most under-utilized technique on the planet. By taking a no-limit attitude, you can achieve anything you desire.

"On thinking time, you never know where the next big idea is going to come from."
Les Hewitt

"You can achieve anything you want."
Dr. Wayne Dyer

I strongly recommend you spend the time to create your own affirmations—that is, your goals and objectives for your life. This needs to be broken down to daily goals for business, health, family, and yourself. Goals can be divided into daily, weekly, quarterly, annually, and 3 to 5 years. Your affirmations must be reasonable and logical. Once you have created your affirmation, you must frequently review it. I recommend you pick a specific time of day – morning works for some and before bedtime works for others – read them daily. And, don't be afraid to ask for what you want! Make sure there is a step-by-step process with precise timeframes to achieve your goals. For example, I break my referrals down to daily goals and weekly goals. I have a specific number of new potential prospects I want to meet in a given period of time and explain to them what I do and how I can help them achieve their dreams and goals.

I once asked for a new top-notch assistant with about 10 qualities that I required for a job opening. Also, I asked for a precise time frame of when this person would be hired in this case no later than March 31st. I asked for this every day for 3 months and in the middle of March I found my person! As part of the interview process, I actually put a list of duties – a job description – in front of a job candidate for the position I wanted to fill and that person remarked, "I don't want to work that hard." Well, that was the end of that interview. When I put the list in front of Delia, the person I eventually hired, she went down the list and said she was comfortable in being able to do the entire task list I required for employment. I am happy to report she is still with me today. You can ask for anything you want. For example, you can ask to go on a vacation in a specific place with a precise price range. You can request a certain very specific type of home with a very specific price range at a very specific time to move into.

When you ask for something and then receive it, this doesn't just magically appear, but comes as a result of asking. Measuring your success is easy; just keep track of your results. I have found that by paying close attention to my affirmations, the universe delivers whatever I ask for. Furthermore, everything builds on momentum. This has greatly reinforced my goals and objectives and has me thinking even bigger.

Another powerful method to use is a picture book, sometimes referred to as "treasure mapping." This can be even more powerful than affirmations because this is a visual picture of your goals and objectives, while affirmations are strictly written words. The materials you will need are: a three-ring binder, lots of construction paper, glue, scissors, red, blue and gold stickers, and at least 10 to 15 magazines. By cutting out pictures and words, you can create your own visual of what you want. You can create a section for family, places you want to go, pages for your kids, material items you wish to buy, and a business section. We review ours quarterly, and now the kids even have their own picture books. When we have accomplished a goal, we put our stickers on them to signify their successful completion. It is amazing how many goals we have achieved since creating our books.

One warning when regarding affirmations and picture books: Only share these with those closest to you. Do not go around advertising to those outside your very tight circle, because those who do not understand these awesome powers will try to use their energies to undermine your goals and objectives.

The Essence of Destiny

"Watch your thoughts, for they become words. Choose your words, for they become actions. Understand your actions, for they become habits. Study your habits, for they will become your character. Develop your character, for it becomes your destiny."

Successories, LLC

Don't be afraid to dream big. Write down what you expect to produce and quantify this by category over the next five years. Review this information on a regular basis and watch how what you have asked for comes true. Get a mentor or a coach to challenge you to take your business to the next level. Believe in yourself! Ask for what you want on a daily basis and watch it happen.

The following are quotes from a variety of people, all of whom have been big thinkers in their lives. I wish you the very best.

Big Thinking Quotes from other Big Thinkers

"Imagination is more important than knowledge." Albert Einstein

"Break your Own Records." Danny Cox, author

"Make the most of yourself, for that is all there is of you." Ralph Waldo Emerson

"A man's life is what his thoughts make of it." Marcus Aurelius

"Pain is temporary; quitting is forever." Lance Armstrong

"As soon as you trust yourself, you will know how to live." Johann Wolfgang Von Goethe (1749-1832), Poet and dramatist

"It's not what happens to you in life that is important. It's how you handle what happens that makes the difference!" MDRT Classic

"When our dreams come true, we have dreamed too little." MDRT Classic

"Change your thoughts and you change the world." Harold R. Mcalindon, Writer

"The only way to discover the limits of the possible is to go beyond them into the impossible." Arthur C. Clarke

"The pursuit of our dreams is, at heart, an act of faith combined with a giant act of will. But when it pays off, the unexpected happens. The world shifts around you, unseen passages open, and in many ways, the rules of reality, at least the rules that have defined your reality, change." Bahram Akradi Founder of Life Time Fitness

"The future is simply infinite possibility waiting to happen. What it waits on is human imagination to crystallize its possibility." Leland Kaiser Motivational Speaker

"I'm looking for a lot of people who have an infinite capacity to not know what can't be done." Henry Ford

"Practice, practice, practice until you eventually get numb on rejection." W. Clement Stone

"You miss 100 percent of the shots you never take." Wayne Gretzky

Recommended Readings

The 21 Laws of Influence by Helen Davis, CLU
Malvern, Pennsylvania. Indaba Press, 2004

The 48 Laws of Power by Robert Green
New York, New York. Penguin Books, 1998

The Aladdin Factor by Jack Canfield and Mark Victor Hansen.
New York, New York. Berkeley Books, Division of Penguin Putnam, 1995

Artful Persuasion by Harry Mills
Broadway, New York. Amacom, 2000

Awaken the Giant Within by Anthony Robbins
New York, New York. Simon and Schuster, 1993

The Celestine Prophecy by James Redfield
New York, New York. Warner Books, Inc, 1993

Dig Your Well Before You're Thirsty by Harvey Mackay
New York, New York. Doubleday, a division of Random House, 1997

Do Less, Achieve More by Chin-Ning Chu
New York, New York. Harper Collins, 1998

Influence and Communication by Helen Davis, CLU
Malvern, Pennsylvania. Indaba Press, 2002

Influence: The Psychology of Persuasion by Robert B. Cialdini, Ph.D. New York, New York. Quill, an imprint of William Morrow & Company, 1984

Life Strategies by Phillip C. McGraw, Ph.D.
New York, New York. Hyperion, 1999

Take Control of Your Subconscious Mind by Anthony T. Galie. Cornerstone Press. Indialantic, Florida, 2000

The Magic of Believing by Claude M. Bristol
New York, New York. Fireside, Published by Simon and Schuster, 1948

The Magic of Thinking Big by David Schwartz, Ph.D.
New York, New York. Fireside, Published by Simon and Schuster, 1959

The Power of Focus by Jack Canfield, Mark Victor Hanson and Les Hewitt. Deerfield Beach, Florida. Health Communications, Inc., 2000

The Richest Man in Babylon by George S. Clason
New American Library, a division of Penguin Putnam Inc. New York, New York, 1926

The Unfair Advantage: Sell With NLP! by Duane Lakin, Ph.D.
Lakin Associates. Wheaton, IL, 2000

The Tipping Point by Malcolm Gladwell
Little, Brown and Company. Boston, Massachusetts, 2000

Think & Grow Rich by Napoleon Hill
Ballantine Publishing Group, a division of Random House, Inc..
New York, New York, 1960

Unlimited Power by Anthony Robbins
Ballantine Books, a division of Random House, Inc. New York, New York, 1986

What to Say When You Talk to Yourself by Shad Helmstetter, Ph.D.
Grindle Press. Scottsdale, Arizona, 1982

Who Are You Really and What Do You Want? by Shad Helmstetter, Ph.D. Park Avenue Press. 2003

You'll See It When You Believe It by Dr. Wayne W. Dyer
Avon Books, an Imprint of Harper Collins Publishers.
New York, New York, 1989

About the Author

For more than a decade, Randy Schuster has been a highly successful financial advisor consistently ranked in the top 5 percent of the profession by the prestigious Million Dollar Round Table (MDRT), the premier association of financial professionals. He has carved out a unique niche within the industry by focusing on the coordination of planning. Randy says, "I am the quarterback and the client is the owner of the team." He guides his clients through the complex tax code in midsize to large estates, planning for business continuation and succession transfers issues of privately held firms, and wealth accumulation strategies. He places a special emphasis on dealing with the *emotional issues* of various family members.

Professional Achievements

Randy has qualified for MDRT for nine consecutive years, during which he has actively volunteered on several committees. He earned MDRT's Court of the Table honors in 2002 and 2003, which represents the top 2 percent of the profession worldwide. In 2004, Randy received Top of the Table honors, which is the top ½ percent of the profession. Randy has been a guest speaker at numerous industry related functions.

Growing Up

Randy was exposed to his own family's transition plan at Marjax Enterprises, a firm founded by his grandfather. In its day, Marjax was a regional powerhouse sporting goods chain in which Randy worked, starting when he was 10 years old. Today, he uses that experience to help owners of family and closely held businesses to develop and implement sound business plans.

Education, Hobbies and Interests

Mr. Schuster earned a B.S. degree in Finance from Indiana University in 1984 and has studied extensively to hold the Certified Coach Executive designation. He also has successfully completed several NASD licenses. He and his wife, Ernestine, reside in Rochester, N.Y., with their two sons, Daniel and Matthew. During his free time, Randy loves to read, play competitive tennis and watch his children play soccer and lacrosse.

For more information on

Randy Schuster

Go to:

Web Site: www.coordinatedplan.com

For details and availability please email.

info@ThePowerOf Habits.com

Or call our office at

585-546-1656

Web Site: www.ThePowerOf Habits.com

Printed in the United States
36897LVS00005B/376-552

9 781585 700011